ESSENTIAL PETS

REPTILES

BY YVETTE LaPIERRE

Essential Library
An Imprint of Abdo Publishing
abdobooks.com

ABDOBOOKS.COM

Published by Abdo Publishing, a division of ABDO, PO Box 398166, Minneapolis, Minnesota 55439.

Printed in the United States of America, North Mankato, Minnesota.
052023
092023

THIS BOOK CONTAINS RECYCLED MATERIALS

Cover Photo: Shutterstock Images (front and back)
Interior Photos: Eric Isselee/Shutterstock Images, 1; Shutterstock Images, 3, 6, 19, 28–29, 32, 37, 50, 54, 90–91, 98, 101; Kuttelvaserova Stuchelova/Shutterstock Images, 4–5; Arie Studio/Shutterstock Images, 8; Jim Wileman/Alamy, 10; Herschel Hoffmeyer/Shutterstock Images, 12–13; Catchlight Lens/Shutterstock Images, 16; Wolfgang Kaehler/LightRocket/Getty Images, 20–21, 21; Cathy Keifer/Shutterstock Images, 23; Shane Myers Photography/Shutterstock Images, 25; Gianluigi Guercia/AFP/Getty Images, 26; AJR Photo/Shutterstock Images, 31; Sidney Photos/Shutterstock Images, 34; B. Stefanov/Shutterstock Images, 40–41; Jasius/Moment/Getty Images, 42; David Kenny/iStockphoto, 44; Sergey and Marina Pyataev/Shutterstock Images, 46; Mark Leung/Shutterstock Images, 52; Bluedog Studio/Shutterstock Images, 57; Africa Studio/Shutterstock Images, 59; Luiza Kleina/Shutterstock Images, 62; Eckehard Schulz/AP Images, 63; Gilbert R. Boucher II/Daily Herald/AP Images, 65; Mark Ralston/AFP/Getty Images, 68, 72; Danny Ye/Shutterstock Images, 70; Owen Humphreys/PA Images/Getty Images, 75; Nynke van Holten/Shutterstock Images, 78–79; US Attorney's Office for the Central District of California/AP Images, 80; Marlonneke Willemsen/Shutterstock Images, 83, 100; Jon G. Fuller/VWPics/AP Images, 84; Florida Fish and Wildlife Conservation Commission/AP Images, 87; Lauren DeCicca/Getty Images News/Getty Images, 95

Editor: Marie Pearson
Series Designer: Becky Daum

Library of Congress Control Number: 2022948877

PUBLISHER'S CATALOGING-IN-PUBLICATION DATA
Names: LaPierre, Yvette, author.
Title: Reptiles / by Yvette LaPierre
Description: Minneapolis, Minnesota: Abdo Publishing Company, 2024 | Series: Essential pets | Includes online resources and index.
Identifiers: ISBN 9781098290559 (lib. bdg.) | ISBN 9781098276737 (ebook)
Subjects: LCSH: Pets--Juvenile literature. | Reptiles as pets--Juvenile literature. | Reptiles--Juvenile literature. | Pets--Behavior--Juvenile literature. | Zoology--Juvenile literature.
Classification: DDC 636.0887--dc23

CONTENTS

CHAPTER 1
A NEW PET 4

CHAPTER 2
NATURAL HISTORY OF REPTILES 12

CHAPTER 3
CHOOSING AND PREPARING FOR REPTILES 28

CHAPTER 4
CARING FOR REPTILES 40

CHAPTER 5
INDUSTRY AND COMMUNITY 54

CHAPTER 6
LAWS AND REGULATIONS 68

CHAPTER 7
REPTILE DEBATES 78

CHAPTER 8
REPTILE OWNERSHIP 90

ESSENTIAL FACTS 100

GLOSSARY 102

ADDITIONAL RESOURCES 104

SOURCE NOTES 106

INDEX 110

ABOUT THE AUTHOR 112

CHAPTER 1

A NEW PET

After many weeks of research and preparation, Diego was finally ready to bring his new bearded dragon home. Diego and his mom had decided a couple of months ago that they would like a pet. They lived in an apartment and were busy with work and school, so they didn't think a dog or a cat would be a good choice. Besides, his grandmother was allergic to many furry pets, and she came to visit often. Diego had always found snakes and lizards to be fascinating animals, so he began reading lots of information about keeping reptiles as pets.

Diego had heard that reptiles were easy pets, but the more he read, the more he realized that reptiles require a lot of specialized care and equipment. All reptiles are ectotherms, or cold-blooded animals. This means that they rely on their surroundings to keep their bodies at the right temperature. In captivity, it is up to the owner

Bearded dragons are the most popular pet reptile in the United States.

to provide the exact temperature, light, and humidity required by a specific reptile. Many reptiles that receive proper care in captivity can live for ten years or more.[1]

Diego decided he was ready for the commitment of caring properly for a reptile for a long time. After reading about many reptiles—from snakes to lizards to turtles—he decided that a type of lizard called a bearded dragon would make a good pet for him. Diego was eager to get his new pet right away, but he knew that he had a lot of work to do first.

The first thing Diego did was check with their landlord to make sure he could keep a reptile in the apartment. The landlord had some rules about reptile ownership, such

A bearded dragon's enclosure should mimic its desert habitat.

as no venomous snakes allowed, but a bearded dragon in an enclosure was permitted. Then Diego checked city and state rules regarding exotic pets and made sure that bearded dragons were permitted.

Next, he located a local exotic pet veterinarian who was qualified to care for reptiles. Dr. Porter agreed that a bearded dragon could make a good pet with proper care. She gave Diego more information about bearded dragon care and recommended some breeders and a local reptile pet rescue that often had reptiles in need of new homes. Diego and his mom visited the reptile rescue center and chose a young bearded dragon. But before they could bring the lizard home, they needed to set up its new home.

Diego bought a large glass tank with a ventilated top. The doors opened to the front and locked so the lizard couldn't escape. He knew the idea was to re-create the bearded dragon's natural habitat as closely as possible. He looked at lots of pictures of bearded dragons in the wild to get inspiration for the enclosure. Bearded dragons are from Australia, where their habitat is sandy, warm, and dry. Diego lined the tank with four inches (10 cm) of special sandy soil.[2] He decorated the enclosure with artificial plants, logs, and branches he purchased at the pet store. That would give his lizard places to hide and to bask in the light. He added a shallow bowl for water. He put special

A baby bearded dragon may be stressed for a few days after being brought home. The owner should monitor it carefully.

lamps for heat and light on top—one for the warm end of the tank and one for the cooler end. Last, Diego put a thermometer on both ends of the tank and a hygrometer to measure humidity. He purchased bearded dragon food that included a variety of insects, plants, and fruit.

Now that everything was ready, Diego and his mom drove to the reptile rescue center. They brought the bearded dragon home in a small carrier. Diego checked the thermometers and hygrometer in the tank one last time. The conditions were just right. The warm end was 105 degrees Fahrenheit (41°C), the cool end was 70 degrees Fahrenheit (21°C), and the humidity was less than 50 percent.[3] He gently placed his new pet in the tank. The lizard paused for a moment, looked at Diego, and then crawled onto a rock to bask under the warm light. Diego was happy to see that his bearded dragon looked right at home.

REPTILES AS PETS

According to a 2021 to 2022 survey, 5.7 million homes in the United States kept at least one reptile as a pet, and the number of reptile pets is growing.[4] There are more than nine million pet reptiles in the United States.[5] Reptile enthusiasts can choose from many varieties of snakes, lizards, turtles, and tortoises. People enjoy reptiles as pets because they are fun to watch and have interesting behaviors. In general, reptiles require less space, exercise, and care than other pets, which can make them good pets for people with busy lifestyles.

That doesn't mean, however, that they are easy to care for. They require very specialized

BEARDED DRAGONS

Bearded dragons are lizards native to the deserts and dry scrublands of eastern and central Australia. A full-grown bearded dragon is about 18 to 24 inches (46–61 cm) long, and most are brown or tan.[6] In the wild, this lizard is active during the day, basking on logs in the sun and hunting insects that it grabs with its sticky tongue. The lizard's beard is a dark flap of skin under its chin that expands when the lizard is threatened to make it look bigger.

housing and care to ensure that they are healthy and thriving. It is up to the pet owner to replicate the reptile's natural environment as closely as possible. That includes the proper enclosure, temperature, lighting, and humidity, as well as a healthy and varied diet. Reptiles can make challenging pets because they rely on their surroundings to stay at the right body temperature. Owners must provide large enclosures with warmer and cooler areas at just the right temperature for the species. In addition, owners should provide items to make the reptile's home stimulating and interesting.

Although reptiles can be a lot of work, many people find owning them a rewarding experience.

It is important to do thorough research before considering buying a reptile pet. Some reptiles do better in captivity than others. Many cities and states require permits for owning some reptiles, and some reptiles are illegal to acquire or move across country or state borders. Most importantly, people should choose only a reptile that has been born and bred in captivity. Extensive capturing of wild reptiles can stress a species' population. Owners should also learn what is known about the reptile's natural environment and gather expert advice on the best care for reptiles. People can research the best reptile breeders and suppliers. Finally, owners should understand the laws regarding trade in reptiles as well as the challenges and benefits of owning a reptile. Doing these things will ensure that reptiles are healthy and safe, both in captivity and in the wild.

IS REPTILE BLOOD COLD?

Reptiles are commonly called cold-blooded animals, but that term can be misleading. Their body temperatures change according to the temperature of the air around them, and their blood is not actually cold all the time. Their body temperature goes up when they bask in the hot sun, and it goes down as they seek shade or during the cool of night. The scientific term for an animal that regulates its body temperature this way, ectotherm, comes from *ectos*, meaning "outside," and *thermos*, meaning "heat."

CHAPTER 2

NATURAL HISTORY OF REPTILES

Reptiles include some of the most ancient animals on Earth. Ancient reptiles began roaming the land more than 300 million years ago. The earliest known reptiles were small, lizard-like animals that lived in forested areas. Over time, many types of reptiles evolved, including ones that walked, swam, and flew. About 230 million years ago, the largest reptiles ever—dinosaurs—appeared. Dinosaurs and other ancient reptiles dominated Earth until most suddenly died out 65 million years ago. The time when dinosaurs were alive is known as the Mesozoic era, or the Age of Reptiles. At the end of this period, dinosaurs and many of these ancient reptiles went extinct. But some smaller reptiles survived. These animals

Some of the dinosaurs were massive. *Tyrannosaurus rex* could weigh up to eight short tons (7.3 metric tons).

gave rise to the more than 10,000 species of reptiles living today.[1]

DINOSAURS

Dinosaurs were a group of ancient reptiles called archosaurs that dominated Earth for more than 140 million years. Some were huge, such as the giant *Spinosaurus*, which weighed an estimated eight short tons (7.3 metric tons).[2] *Microraptor*, on the other hand, was the size of a chicken. Dinosaurs weren't the only ancient reptiles, though. Large reptiles that are now extinct swam through ancient waters and flew through the air.

REPTILES TODAY

Reptiles are one of the most diverse groups of organisms. They have evolved different adaptations to live in almost every ecosystem on the planet. They exist everywhere on Earth except the North and South Poles. They have adapted to live in many habitats, from the open sea to mountains, forests, grasslands, and deserts. There are four groups of reptiles: snakes and lizards, crocodiles, turtles (including tortoises), and the tuatara, a rare reptile found only in New Zealand.

As a group, they have many body types, ranging from long, legless snakes to four-legged turtles with large shells. Reptiles can slither, walk on four feet, or run on two feet. They can climb trees and branches and cling to smooth walls or hang upside down from ceilings. Some can even glide through the air. The smallest reptiles can be less than one inch (2.5 cm) long as adults, while some pythons and crocodiles may grow to more than 23 feet (7 m) long.[3] Their life spans are equally diverse. Some small reptiles may live only a year or two. However, most live at least ten years. Some, such as loggerhead sea turtles and giant tortoises, live 50 years or more in the wild.[4]

Despite all these differences, however, reptiles have some things in common. All reptiles are vertebrates with tails. Contrary to popular belief, reptiles are not slimy. They have thick, dry skin that is covered in scales. The scales covering a reptile's dry skin are made out of keratin, which is the same tough material in human hair and fingernails. These scales may be tiny or large, depending on the size of the reptile. The shells of turtles and tortoises are covered in large scales. These hard scales are also known as scutes. The thick skin of reptiles doesn't stretch. When a reptile outgrows its skin, it sheds the old skin and grows a new one.

All reptiles are ectotherms. To warm

CHANGING NUMBERS

The number of living reptile species can change from year to year. Sometimes the number gets smaller due to the extinction of species. But sometimes the number rises due to discoveries of new species. In 2010, scientists found a big, fruit-eating monitor lizard in the Philippines. While it was unknown to science before then, it was familiar to many local people. In 2005, researchers found the horned anole living in Ecuador. This long-nosed lizard was thought to be extinct.

up, a reptile may bask on a rock in the hot sun. If a reptile needs to cool its body temperature, it may burrow under soil or seek shade.

Most reptiles are hatched from eggs. Reptiles build nests or dig holes in warm sand or soil to lay eggs. When the eggs are ready to hatch, baby reptiles use a special pointed egg tooth to break through the shell. Soon after, the egg tooth falls off. A few snakes and lizards are born live from eggs that hatch inside their mother's body.

Almost all reptiles eat some form of animal life, including insects, mammals, birds, frogs, fish, and even other reptiles. Some land tortoises are herbivores.

Crocodiles are among the few reptile species whose mothers care for their young after hatching.

Depending on the habitat, they may eat leaves, grasses, or cacti.

SNAKES

According to the fossil record, the first snakes appeared as far back as 167 million years ago. Today there are about 3,500 species of snakes.[5] They occupy a variety of habitats, from deserts to rain forests. They make their homes on land, underground, in trees, and in lakes and oceans.

REPTILE COMMUNICATION

Reptiles can communicate with each other in a number of ways. Some snakes and lizards spread chemical odors to send messages. Then other reptiles use their tongues to smell the messages. Male spiny lizards use push-ups, which are an up-and-down motion of the front end, to warn away other lizards or impress a female. A few reptile species use vocal communication. For example, the tokay gecko from Southeast Asia has a number of vocalizations, from quiet chirps to loud calls. Males loudly call "Geck-oh" to attract females. That's how the species got its scientific name, *Gekko gecko*.

Like all reptiles, snakes' scaly skin is dry and smooth. Their skin comes in a variety of colors and patterns to help them blend in with their surroundings. Snakes shed their skins as they grow.

Snakes are generally legless, though a few can grow partial, typically useless hind legs. Snakes have long, flexible spines that contain between 120 and 500 bones, depending on how big the snake is.[6] A pair of ribs attaches to each of these bones and supports strong muscles.

Scales on the belly give a snake traction on a surface. The strong, flexible spine allows them to slither back and forth swiftly across land and in water. The flexible spine also allows snakes to swallow large prey.

While most snakes slither on land, five species of snakes glide through the air. They are known as flying or gliding snakes and live in the jungles, forests, and woodlands of South and Southeast Asia. A gliding snake climbs a tree using a ridge of scales along its belly. When it reaches the end of a branch, the snake flings itself to a lower branch of another tree. The snake flattens its body, making its underside curve up into the body so it acts like a parachute.

Snakes don't have eyelids or outer ears. The bones in their bodies feel slight vibrations in the ground and carry that information to the inner ears in their skulls, allowing them to detect nearby prey or predators. Snakes have long, forked tongues, which they use to touch and smell their surroundings. By licking the air, snakes' sensitive tongues pick up smells of nearby prey. They use their tongues to follow scent trails to their next meals.

All snakes are carnivores. They eat a variety of animals, including insects, frogs, and small and large mammals. Depending on the type of snake, they may kill their prey by poisoning, squeezing, or simply grabbing and swallowing it. Many catch their prey by gripping it with

Owners should provide their snakes with objects such as driftwood that the snakes can rub against to help remove their shedding skin.

their sharp teeth. Some snakes, such as boas, pythons, and anacondas, are known as constrictors. They grab prey in their jaws and then wrap around the animal and slowly squeeze it to death. Venomous snakes bite their prey and pump venom through hollow fangs to subdue the animal. Snakes do not chew their meals but swallow them whole by unhinging their jaws and stretching their mouths wide. Their flexible spines allow them to swallow and digest animals much larger than themselves. A large python, for example, can swallow an adult deer. After a very big meal, some snakes can go many months without eating again.

PYTHONS IN BENIN

In the West African country of Benin, royal pythons, also known as ball pythons, have their own temple in the city of Ouidah. Dozens of pythons slither freely around the Temple of Pythons, where the snakes are housed and worshipped. According to legend, the worship of pythons began after a war in 1717 when the kingdom of Ouidah was defeated. The defeated king took refuge in a big forest. As his enemies searched the woods, many pythons started to crawl out of the forest, protecting the king from capture. The king decided to honor the pythons by building three huts in the forest as a temple to commemorate them. Throughout Ouidah and other parts of the country, pythons are symbols of peace, prosperity, and wisdom.

About 60 pythons now make their home in the temple, though they sometimes wander into local homes where they are welcomed before being returned to

People are allowed to hold the pythons at Ouidah. The snakes have great significance for people who follow the religion Vodun.

the temple.[7] Guides welcome visitors to the temple and lead them on tours to see the historic huts and the pythons they care for. Visitors are allowed to pick up and take pictures with the snakes, and it's encouraged to tip the guide as a token of appreciation.

LIZARDS

Lizards are the largest group of reptiles, with at least 6,500 species, including geckos, chameleons, and iguanas.[8] There are more species of lizards than of mammals, and new ones occasionally are discovered. Lizards have the greatest diversity of habitat, shape, size, and behavior of all reptile groups. Most lizards live in warm regions, but they survive and thrive from the southern tip of South America to near the Arctic Circle. They live in forests, deserts, and even salt water. Some are good at climbing, and some dig burrows or swim.

Most lizards have four legs and a long tail. Some, such as the worm lizards of Mexico, have no legs. Some lizards can stand upright on two back legs and run. Still others, known as flying lizards, can spread out a fold of skin like wings, catch the wind, and glide through the air from tree to tree. Many lizards have the amazing ability to detach their tails when attacked. The dropped tail keeps wriggling, confusing the predator. Most lizards then regrow a new tail.

Lizards come in many shapes and sizes. The smallest is the nano-chameleon, which is less than one inch (2.5 cm) long when fully grown. The largest lizard is the Komodo dragon, which can grow up to 10 feet (3 m) long.[9] Lizards come in just about every color and pattern imaginable, and some lizards can change their color.

Lizards have eyelids, unlike snakes. But like snakes, they use their tongues to sense their surroundings. Their tongues gather information to help them find food and mates and warn them if a predator is nearby. Lizard tongues are useful in other ways too. Lizards can use their long, sticky tongues to snag insects out of the air. Geckos use their tongues to clean their faces, including their eyes.

Most lizards are carnivorous. They eat animals appropriate to their size, from insects to mammals. Some lizards are omnivorous. They eat animals as well as fruits

Chameleons can change the colors of their skin as a way to communicate with other chameleons.

and vegetables. Most lizards live about five years in the wild but can live much longer than that in captivity.

TURTLES AND TORTOISES

Turtles are the only reptiles with shells. They evolved about 250 million years ago and have remained relatively unchanged since then. They are the second-largest order of reptiles after lizards. More than 300 species of turtles are known.[10] Some turtles live entirely on land, while others live entirely in the water or partially on land and partially in the water. Tortoises are a type of turtle that lives only on land.

The shell is both shelter and protection for turtles and tortoises. When threatened, a turtle retreats into its shell. Some can completely close their shells. The shell is part of its skeleton and is made up of two parts. The top curved part is called the carapace.

CHANGING COLORS

Many reptiles are shades of brown or green, but some are very colorful. Some lizards can even change color. Geckos can lighten or darken their skin color as their environment changes. Many lizards can change their color to match their surroundings. That allows them to hide from predators or sneak up on their prey. A chameleon can change its color based on changes in temperature, the environment, or even its mood. A panther chameleon, for example, may start out blue but shift to green, then yellow, then orange, and finally to red as it gets more upset.

The flatter underside is called the plastron. Most have a shell covered by scales known as scutes. Each species of turtle has its own scute pattern. The shell pattern grows as the reptile does. Tortoises tend to have larger and more rounded shells than many other turtles. Many turtle and tortoise shells are big and strong. Some sea turtles have developed lighter, more streamlined shells for their lives in the ocean.

Turtles have movable eyelids, like lizards. Like snakes, they don't have external ears. Unlike both of those groups, turtles and tortoises don't have teeth. Instead, they have beak-like jaws that chomp up plants and small animals into bite-size pieces. Many turtles are omnivores.

Sea turtles can migrate thousands of miles across the ocean between feeding and breeding grounds.

Jonathan, a Seychelles giant tortoise who is housed on the island of Saint Helena, turned 190 in 2022. He was the oldest known land animal at the time.

These slow-moving reptiles eat slow-moving prey, such as worms and insects.

Large land tortoises are mainly vegetarians. Turtles range in size from tiny speckled tortoises that weigh 3.5 ounces (100 g) to huge leatherback sea turtles weighing more than 1,760 pounds (800 kg).[11] In the wild, turtles regularly live 20 to 30 years or more, and sea turtles have life spans of 60 to 70 years. A few tortoise species have lived 100 years or more in captivity.[12]

HISTORY OF REPTILES AS PETS

Pictures of cobras and crocodiles at a cemetery in Egypt from approximately 2500 BCE may be the earliest records of captive reptiles in the world. The London Zoo in England became the first zoo to open a reptile building in 1849. In the late 1800s, a number of books were published in Victorian England describing the care of captive reptiles. Private reptile keepers in England, many of whom were women, used these books, but they also made their own discoveries and innovations in the care of captive reptiles. These private keepers and zoos with reptiles exchanged information and learned from each other. Zoos and private owners kept monitor lizards, tegus, bearded dragons, anoles, chameleons, and more.

In the United States, reptiles began to gain popularity as pets following World War II (1939–1945). Since then, the number of reptiles in captivity has risen, particularly since the 1990s. In 2007, reptiles were kept as pets in 2 percent of US households. That had more than doubled to 4.5 percent of households by 2020.[13] From the 1940s to the 1970s, most reptiles sold in the United States were native species collected from the wild, such as red-eared slider turtles, green anoles, and hatchling turtles. During the latter half of the 1900s, reptiles were regularly imported from Australia, Africa, South and Central America, and Asia for the pet trade. Today, many reptile enthusiasts and conservationists promote captive breeding of reptiles for pets instead of purchasing animals captured from the wild, though wild-caught species continue to be traded.

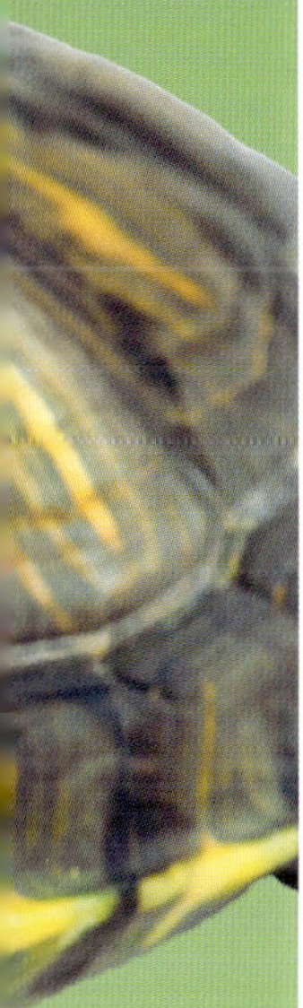

CHAPTER 3

CHOOSING AND PREPARING FOR REPTILES

The first and most important step in reptile care is research. Before buying or adopting a reptile pet, an owner must research the many types of reptiles to determine which would be the best choice given their ability to properly care for it. Some reptile species are better suited for first-time reptile owners, while others present more challenges and are better suited to experienced handlers. All reptiles need proper housing and food, but each species will have very specific care needs. Also, it is the pet owner's responsibility to check local, state, and federal laws to ensure that the desired reptile is allowed

The semiaquatic red-eared slider turtle needs a very different enclosure than what desert reptiles need.

and to determine whether a special permit is needed for ownership. Finally, new owners should find a local veterinarian who is trained in reptile care. The veterinarian and other trusted resources are the best sources of information on reptile care.

CHOOSING A REPTILE PET

Potential reptile owners should ask some important questions when choosing a new pet, such as how long the animal will live. Many lizards and snakes live for ten to 15 years in captivity.[1] Some larger snakes and tortoises can live significantly longer. An owner must be prepared for the commitment of caring for a pet during its entire life span. Also, owners should consider how large the animal will grow. Some reptiles will stay relatively small, while others may grow many times larger than their juvenile size. For example, some iguanas grow to three or four feet (0.9–1.2 m) long and may be difficult to handle when they reach this size.[2]

Another consideration is how much it will cost to acquire, feed, and care for the animal over its life span. These costs will vary widely between species. Owners should be comfortable with the care needs, such as feeding live insects or frozen animals to a pet. Additionally, potential buyers should ask if the reptile is safe for the household. Some reptiles are more aggressive than others,

Iguanas grow into large, powerful animals. They may need custom enclosures so they have enough space.

especially if they grow large, and may bite. In addition, some reptiles carry bacteria that are harmful to humans. For this reason, reptiles are not recommended for homes with very young children or for people with compromised immune systems.

BASIC REPTILE CARE

All reptiles require an enclosure of the proper size and type. Large terrestrial turtles and tortoises may be housed in an outdoor pen if the climate is appropriate for the species. But many reptiles require an indoor glass tank, also known as a vivarium. The vivarium must be

Reptiles that climb need branches and other items to climb on. These pets need ventilated tops that have holes too small for them to escape.

large enough for the fully grown animal to move, crawl, or slither around, with areas to bask in light or hide in shade to regulate body temperature. A snake will need a long tank, while a tree-climbing gecko will require a tall vivarium. The tank should have good ventilation and secure latches.

The vivarium needs to be lined on the bottom with substrate, or bedding. The type and amount of substrate depends on the reptile species' natural environment. For example, a reptile that naturally lives in the desert requires a sandy bedding, while a jungle-dwelling species would need a soft, deep soil. A variety of substrates for reptiles are available, including indoor-outdoor carpet, mulched wood, coconut husks, moss, and fine sand. Owners should use fine sand that is marketed specially for reptiles. Play sand or construction sand can have large, sharp particles that can injure the pets.

Using the wrong bedding can be life-threatening. For example, sandy soil is not good for insectivores such as young bearded dragons. They might eat the sand along with their insect food, which can clog their intestines. Bedding like bark that traps moisture is not good for desert-dwelling reptiles. The high humidity can lead to respiratory problems. A reputable reptile care guide or veterinarian can help with making the right selection. The bedding should be cleaned regularly. Reptiles like plants, branches, rocks, and other furnishings. These enrichment items allow the animals to dig, hide, and climb, just as they would in their natural habitats.

Each species of reptile requires specific temperatures, and many need separate hot, warm, and cool areas in the enclosure. Warmth can be provided by heat lamps or heat pads. The vivarium should have one or more thermometers to measure the temperature at different ends of the tank. Reptiles need about 12 hours of light.[3] Natural sunlight is best, but reptile owners can also use artificial lights that mimic sunlight. Natural sunlight includes infrared and ultraviolet light. Ultraviolet light includes ultraviolet A (UVA), ultraviolet B (UVB), and ultraviolet C (UVC) light. Light needs vary according to the species, but most need infrared, UVA, and UVB light. Infrared light provides warmth and is absorbed through the reptile's skin. UVA light is essential to support reptiles' extremely good color vision. Reptiles, in fact, see a more colorful rainbow than humans do. UVB lighting helps promote a healthy immune system.

In addition, most reptiles need a particular amount of humidity to keep them healthy and to help them shed

There are different styles of basking lights. Some hang over a reptile's enclosure.

their skin. Humidity levels depend on the species and may be provided by shallow bowls of water or regular spraying with a spray bottle. Heat lamps, substrate that holds little water, and well-ventilated tanks keep humidity low. Each enclosure should have a hygrometer to monitor humidity. Detailed care guides or a veterinarian can explain the specific heat, lighting, and humidity needs of a particular reptile.

Reptiles need nutritious and varied diets that depend on the species. All snakes are carnivores, and some require live food. Lizards, turtles, and tortoises may be herbivores or insectivores. Some species are omnivores. The amount and frequency of feeding varies greatly by species. A small lizard may eat every day, larger lizards and snakes twice a week, and very big snakes only once every two to four weeks.[4]

NO ROOMMATES

Most reptiles should be housed alone. Many reptiles are solitary animals and prefer living by themselves. Some, such as bearded dragons, are territorial rather than social. Keeping multiple lizards in one enclosure may lead to fighting and injuries. Even if two reptiles don't fight, one may eat most of the food while the other goes hungry. In general, reptiles live longer, healthier lives without roommates.

All reptiles should have access to fresh water. Some like to soak, others drink from a shallow bowl, and some sip drops from leaves. Tap water is best.

Distilled or softened water lacks the minerals reptiles need. Depending on its quality, some tap water could need to be conditioned to remove chlorine and other chemicals that may be added to city water sources.

HANDLING REPTILES

Handling a reptile can be a way to bond and interact with the animal. It also can be an important method of examining a reptile to assess its physical health. Regular handling of a reptile pet also can prepare it for a visit to the veterinarian. Some reptiles, however, are more comfortable with being handled than others. Some lizard and snake species can be held without stressing or injuring the reptile. Young slider turtles, on the other hand, should not be held or petted except as necessary because they are fragile and can be easily hurt.

Owners should always consider the behavior of the reptile before handling it. If the animal is in the open and appears calm, it may be a good time to interact. Reptiles that are hiding, moving quickly, or showing other signs of stress should be left alone. People should never surprise a reptile with a quick grab or force it to be picked up, except in an emergency. Many reptiles dislike being handled and may be stressed by direct interaction with an owner. Feeding, misting, and observing are often the best ways to interact with a reptile.

Some owners hand-feed their reptiles as a way to interact with them and build trust.

It's also important to keep in mind how long the reptile is out of its enclosure. The temperature and humidity outside the tank may be very different and harmful for the reptile if it is left out too long. After about ten to 15 minutes of handling, owners should return the reptile to its tank.[5]

VET CARE

All pets, including reptiles, need regular visits to a veterinarian to ensure they are healthy and for early detection and treatment of illnesses. Not all vets are trained to care for reptiles, so it is important to check the qualifications of a vet before scheduling a visit. People can search for reptile vets through the Association of Reptile and Amphibian Veterinarians (ARAV). Owners should take their new reptile to the vet shortly after getting it. On this first visit, the vet will perform a physical exam and conduct tests to assess the reptile's health and look for signs of disease. The visit should also include a thorough discussion of proper feeding, housing, and care of the pet. Owners can ask the vet any questions they might have.

EXOTIC VETS

Reptile medicine has become a specialized area of veterinary training, and these vet specialists have the knowledge they need to recognize and treat reptile illnesses and injuries. When choosing a vet for a reptile, owners can ask about the vet's experiences and qualifications for treating reptiles. Many will be members of the ARAV. This organization promotes better understanding of reptile medical care.

Reptiles should see the vet for a wellness exam at least once a year. Owners should also look for signs of illness, injury, or unhealthy behaviors and bring their pet to the vet if they observe any. Some common illnesses and conditions include dehydration, anorexia, retention of shed skin, and metabolic bone disease. All of these are generally the result of improper housing, environment, and diet. Owners should keep an eye out for abnormal swelling and for burns, which are a result of reptiles lying on unprotected heat pads or climbing too close to a heat lamp. Behaviors that might indicate a reptile is ill or stressed include too little activity; too much activity, such as persistent climbing or crawling around the tank; or eating non-food materials, such as the bedding.

Pet owners can discuss the potential need for spaying and neutering with a vet, since their needs are different than those of mammals. For example, in lizards, the removal of the male reproductive organs requires a major abdominal surgery, so owners should weigh the pros and cons with a veterinarian. Neutering is most common in large male iguanas to try to reduce hormonal, aggressive behavior. The surgery may be too stressful for some more sensitive lizards, such as chameleons. Spaying female lizards is more routine but should be done by a reptile vet.

METABOLIC BONE DISEASE

Metabolic bone disease is the most common problem seen in lizards. It is not a single disease but a collection of disorders that result from the improper care and feeding of reptiles. In general, reptiles develop metabolic bone disease when their diet lacks enough calcium. Another cause is the lack of vitamin D due to insufficient UV lighting. Lizards with metabolic bone disease develop weak bones, fractures, and swollen jaws. Owners can provide correct lighting and sprinkle a calcium supplement on their pets' food to help prevent metabolic bone disease.

CHAPTER 4

CARING FOR REPTILES

In some ways, all reptiles have similar care needs because they are all ectotherms. Each group of reptiles, however, has its own specific needs. And within those groups, the needs of different species and subspecies change. For example, a small corn snake native to shrublands in the United States is cared for very differently than a 20-foot (6 m) python native to Southeast Asia. Owners should consult guides dedicated to the species they own for the very specific care needs of that species.

SNAKE CARE

Snakes that are good choices for newer reptile enthusiasts include corn snakes, ball pythons, and rosy boas. These snakes generally are calm but active, have relatively basic care requirements,

A corn snake can live ten to 15 years. Females grow larger than males.

The rosy boa is popular for its many colors and patterns, which can include stripes that run down the length of the snake's body.

and adapt well to captivity. They are readily available as captive-bred animals, and some have been bred to have a range of morphs, a term for colors and patterns.

Among the most challenging snakes are anacondas, Burmese pythons, reticulated pythons, and African rock pythons. These species can grow very big and be dangerous. A few kept as pets have constricted and killed their owners. Most states restrict or prohibit owning them as pets. In addition, people should avoid keeping venomous snakes as pets because of the danger they pose to their keepers and to others if they escape.

A pet snake requires a glass tank that is long enough to allow the snake to move freely and that provides warmer and cooler areas to help the snake regulate its body temperature. The tank should be at least as long as the snake will be when fully grown, and at least as wide and as tall as half the snake's length. When in doubt, bigger is better so that the snake will have plenty of room to exercise. The enclosure should have secure lid latches because snakes can be talented escape artists.

The tank should be lined with the bedding that best mimics the snake's natural habitat. For example, corn snakes like to burrow, so a thick layer of coconut fiber or appropriate soil is best. Rosy boas need sand or sandy soil similar to their natural habitat in deserts and dry areas. Owners need to clean the bedding regularly to help keep the snakes healthy. Snakes like places to hide and climb, so owners can decorate the tank with rocks, branches, artificial plants, and hiding spots like cardboard tubes. Additionally, a snake needs a heavy water dish with water for drinking and soaking, depending on the snake. The water should be replaced with fresh water daily.

Snakes in captivity need a distinct cycle of day and night, just as they would have in the wild. Owners should provide plenty of sunlight or artificial lighting that mimics sunlight, and they should replace bulbs every year. Most snakes require two or three different temperature zones, so if natural sunlight is used, only part of the vivarium should be in direct sunlight. For example, corn snakes like a warm basking area that is 90 degrees Fahrenheit (32°C) and a cool zone that is about 75 degrees Fahrenheit (24°C). Night temperatures should not fall below 68 degrees Fahrenheit (20°C).[1] Heat bulbs in special dome lamps should sit on top of the tank at each end and, in most cases, should be turned off at night to mimic the cool night air.

Humidity levels depend on the species. Ball pythons need areas of higher and lower humidity, ranging from

Brazilian rainbow boas need a vivarium that mimics the humid, tropical climate of the forests they live in.

45 to 75 percent.[2] Corn snakes thrive at humidity levels between 65 and 75 percent.[3] Rosy boas should be kept below 60 percent.[4] Owners should mist the enclosures daily for snakes that like higher humidity.

All snakes are carnivorous. Young corn snakes eat newborn mice, known as pinkies, and as they grow they can eat adult mice. Ball pythons eat mice, rats, gerbils, and birds. Many snakes can be trained to eat pre-killed rodents that are purchased frozen and thawed before feeding. This is more humane for the prey and safer for the snake than stunning a live rodent before dropping it into the tank. Live prey can bite a snake, and even a minor wound can become infected.

CORN SNAKES

Corn snakes are native to the southeastern United States and parts of Mexico and the Cayman Islands, and they live in forests, meadows, and even abandoned houses, spending most of their time on the ground. They got their name because early European farmers in the United States found them in corn fields and corn storage buildings. The farmers feared the snakes were eating their corn, but the snakes were helping the farmers by eating the rodents that like to eat corn.

Certain types of snakes may need their food dusted with vitamin supplements. Some people drop the food into the snake's tank. But others feed their snakes using small tongs or forceps. Gripping the prey with the tongs, they can wiggle the food a bit to mimic how prey might

Blue-tongued skinks are named for the color of their tongues. They live mainly on the ground.

move in the wild. This encourages the snake to strike and gives it a way to practice a natural behavior.

LIZARDS

Popular pet lizards include blue-tongued skinks, bearded dragons, leopard geckos, and crested geckos. All these lizards are small- to medium-sized, are gentler than other reptiles, and have basic care requirements. More challenging types include iguanas, monitor lizards, and tegu lizards. All these species grow quite large and can be difficult to handle and even aggressive as adults. They require very large enclosures with quality lighting and varied diets. These lizards are restricted or illegal in many states because they have become invasive in parts of the United States.

Each lizard species needs the correct size and style of enclosure with proper levels of light, heat, and humidity, and typically there should be just one lizard per enclosure. Blue-tongued skinks, for example, are active and love to explore. This lizard needs an enclosure that is at least 120 gallons (454 L), though the bigger the better.[5] Blue-tongued skinks like to burrow, so the vivarium should be lined with deep, soft bedding. Bearded dragons and leopard geckos are native to drier climates like deserts and scrublands. Their enclosures should be large enough for the lizard to get plenty of activity, and they should be lined with a sandy substrate. Crested geckos are tree-dwelling lizards in the wild, so their enclosures should be tall with lots of things to climb.

Ideal temperature, light, and humidity levels are specific to each species. Blue-tongued skinks like a warmer, drier area and a cooler, more humid area in the vivarium. These lizards are active during the day, so they need plenty of sunlight or reptile lights and heating bulbs. The basking area should be 105 to 115 degrees Fahrenheit (41–46°C).[6] Proper humidity levels vary depending on the subspecies of skink, ranging from 40 to 80 percent. Leopard geckos need lots of light and warm temperatures, but their humidity level should be kept below 50 percent.

SKINKS

Compared with other lizards, skinks have short necks, stubby legs, and heavy bodies. They tend to move more slowly than other lizards and don't like to climb. There are more than 1,500 species of skinks divided into different groups, including many varieties of blue-tongued skinks.[9] Though they differ in size and color, all blue-tongued skinks have, as the name implies, a distinctive berry-blue tongue. Captive blue-tongued skinks can live 15 to 20 years or more.[10]

Crested geckos don't require such warm temperatures, but they do need lots of humidity. Owners should thoroughly spray down a crested gecko's enclosure twice a day to keep the humidity between 60 and 80 percent at all times.[7]

Many lizard species are omnivores and do best with a variety of foods, as well as access to clean, fresh water. Blue-tongued skinks eat vegetables, fruits, and insects. Half of their diets should be protein. Bearded dragons and leopard geckos eat a variety of insects, including crickets, locusts, mealworms, and waxworms, along with the occasional greens. Food should be dusted with calcium supplements.

Crested geckos eat mostly fruits and insects in the wild. In captivity, they should be fed special diet powders containing ground insects and fruit, mixed with water. Some crested geckos also like to hunt and eat live crickets. With proper care, bearded dragons live ten to 15 years and geckos 15 to 20 years in captivity.[8]

TURTLES AND TORTOISES

Most turtle and tortoise species have relatively challenging care requirements. Many turtles need very large enclosures, and some grow so large that it's impractical to keep them indoors. For example, African spurred tortoises, also known as Sulcata tortoises, are readily available for purchase when small. But these tortoises can grow to weigh more than 100 pounds (45 kg) and need very large enclosures.

Regulating the light, temperature, and humidity levels in big enclosures, especially outdoor ones, is challenging and requires careful monitoring. In addition, theses reptiles require a major owner commitment as they can live 70 years or longer.[11] Turtles that are a little easier to care for include box turtles and Russian tortoises, though compared with other reptiles, they still require an intermediate level of care.

Turtles may be terrestrial, aquatic, or semiaquatic, and this determines the enclosure setup. Terrestrial, or land, turtles and tortoises need large enclosures that allow them to move freely for exercise. Large turtles and tortoises may need a large outdoor pen rather than a tank indoors. Outdoor pens should be placed in an area that has well-draining soil and access to both sun and shade throughout the day. Depending on the species and where a person lives, keeping a turtle outside all year

REPTILE SPOTLIGHT

RUSSIAN TORTOISE

Russian tortoises are native to central Asia, where they live in the dry, sandy deserts of Kazakhstan, Uzbekistan, Turkmenistan, Kyrgyzstan, Afghanistan, and the northeastern edge of Iran. They spend most of their time near water sources where they have access to lots of vegetation. The Russian tortoise is also known as the Afghan tortoise, Horsfield's tortoise, four-toed tortoise, and steppe tortoise.

Russian tortoises grow to about five to ten inches (13–25 cm) long, and the females are larger than the males.[12] They have oval, somewhat flattened shells and big scales on their feet and tails. Their coloring is generally olive or yellow-brown with a dark spot on each scute.

Russian tortoises are hardy animals, but they have specific care needs. They need a very large enclosure, ideally outdoors whenever possible, with sunny and shady areas and a large, shallow saucer of clean water. If cared for properly, a pet Russian tortoise can live 50 years or more, so they are high-commitment pets.[13]

may not be possible. Potential owners should research the species and determine if they need to prepare an indoor enclosure in addition to an outdoor area for cooler weather. They may instead need to choose a smaller species that can be kept indoors more easily.

Land turtles and tortoises should have proper bedding, shaded areas, and a large, shallow bowl of clean water. Each species needs the right levels of light, heat, and humidity to ensure good health. Tropical turtles need warm temperatures and very high levels of humidity. Box turtles native to the eastern United States like temperatures up to 88 degrees Fahrenheit (31°C) and 60 to 80 percent humidity.[14] A Russian tortoise prefers basking temperatures as high as 95 degrees Fahrenheit (35°C) and humidity levels up to 75 percent.[15] Even though these tortoises live in dry areas with sandy soil and sparse vegetation naturally, they spend a lot of time in burrows that are moist.

Aquatic turtles require tanks with special underwater heaters, heat lamps, and basking lamps. The size of the tank depends on the turtle. The tank size should be at least ten gallons (38 L) of water for every inch (2.5 cm) of the turtle's shell length.[16] Turtles are good climbers, so the tank should be tall enough that the turtle can't climb out. A good rule is to have at least one turtle body length between the surface of the water and

Water needs to be deep enough for the turtle to swim fully underwater.

the top of the enclosure. A screen on the top can help prevent escapes.

Good quality water is important for the turtle's health. Water should be dechlorinated before adding it to the tank. High quality water filters will keep the water clean and keep toxins such as ammonia from building up in the water. Owners should replace one-quarter to one-half of the tank's water every week.[17] They should completely replace the water at least once a month or more as needed. If the water looks and smells dirty, it is past time to change the water. It is best to keep the water clean so that doesn't happen.

Many aquatic turtles spend some time out of the water basking, so the tank should include rocks that rise out of the water. Owners can provide tunnels and logs for turtles to hide underneath and climb on. It is very important, however, to ensure that the turtle can't get stuck or trapped underwater. Aquatic plants can also enrich the tank, but the plants must be safe for the species to eat because aquatic turtles often eat vegetation. Safe plants include duckweed, water lily, water lettuce, water fern, and water hyacinth.

Most tortoises are herbivores and should be provided a variety of fresh fruits, vegetables, grasses, leaves, and edible flowers daily. Many turtles, such as eastern box turtles, eat both plants and animals. Their diet should be about half plants such as lettuce and berries and half insects, small pre-killed animals, and special turtle pellets. Turtles and tortoises should be housed alone. They generally don't like being handled and may bite when frightened. Even though they don't have teeth, their bite can hurt.

WHAT'S THE DIFFERENCE?

The turtle family of reptiles includes turtles, tortoises, and terrapins. Tortoises spend most of their time on land, walking on stumpy feet. Turtles have webbed feet and spend most of their time in water, including lakes, rivers, ponds, and streams. However, some turtles, such as box turtles, live mainly on land. Sea turtles live in the ocean. Terrapins are a type of turtle that lives in and near salt water and salt marshes along the East Coast of North America. Terrapins live both on land and in the water and are never far from a water source when on land.

CHAPTER 5

INDUSTRY AND COMMUNITY

Reptiles increased in popularity as pets in the 2010s. As a result, the pet care industry is booming. In 2019, Americans spent $495 million on purchasing reptile products.[1] That number continued to grow into 2022. Organizations, publications, and social media groups that provide education, support, and community for reptile enthusiasts are also a part of the reptile business.

SUPPLIERS AND BREEDERS

Reptiles can be purchased many places, including from pet stores, individuals, and reptile breeders. Reptiles also are offered for sale at flea markets, by street vendors, at herpetology fairs, and, increasingly, through the internet. It is generally not a good idea to purchase a reptile from an individual with no credentials through a classified ad or at a flea market. These reptiles often

Pet stores are some of the most common places for people to purchase reptiles. But people can also go directly to breeders.

come with a host of health problems from improper care. The best places to purchase reptiles are reputable pet stores and breeders. Pet stores that sell reptiles include well-known chains such as Petco and PetSmart. There are also pet stores that specialize in reptiles throughout the United States. In addition, reptiles can be purchased from online stores, such as MorphMarket, and at the North American Reptile Breeders Conference & Trade Shows.

To determine if a supplier or breeder has a good reputation, prospective owners should do some research. They should visit the pet stores they are interested in shopping at and observe the reptiles there. Buyers can use what they know about each reptile species' equipment and care needs and compare that with its environment at the store. They should ask whether the enclosure is the right size and type and if it is clean. They should check if there are there too many reptiles crowded together in one tank.

The enclosures should have thermometers and hygrometers measuring the current temperatures and humidity, and there should be enrichment items for the animals. The reptiles should be behaving like healthy animals and be clean with bright eyes. Buyers can check for signs of parasites, abnormal swellings, or injuries. They can ask about the diet, how often the reptile is handled, and where the reptile was born and bred.

Potential buyers should do their best to determine if a breeder is taking good care of their animals.

When choosing a breeder, potential pet buyers can read reviews and testimonials of customers who have purchased reptiles there. They can also check online reptile forums, Facebook groups, and reptile publications for more information on specific breeders. Buyers can reach out to the breeder for more information and ask the breeder for references from previous buyers. The breeder should be willing to answer all a buyer's questions and provide more information and photos. Most reputable breeders ship reptiles across the country and provide a guarantee for a healthy pet on arrival. Many also provide ongoing advice and support for customers. When it comes to purchasing reptiles, people should make the effort to be informed and buy responsibly.

MORPHMARKET

MorphMarket is an online marketplace that connects reptile and amphibian sellers and buyers. With more than 3,000 breeders worldwide represented, it is the largest reptile marketplace in the world.[2] In December 2022, more than 218,000 animals were for sale.[3] The site requires users to agree to its code of ethics, which states that keepers should be knowledgeable about the species they are buying and that sellers must make an effort to ensure that a buyer understands the care an animal will need. As with all reptile purchases, it's a good idea to read information and reviews before contacting a specific seller or breeder, especially since there can be scammers who might just take a buyer's money.

ENCLOSURES, FOOD, AND MORE

Besides the reptiles themselves, there are many supplies that owners need to buy. An industry exists to provide these items. Pet stores offer reptile products in their stores and online. Other online stores in North America that specialize in reptile supplies and enclosures include Reptile Supply Company, ReptilesRuS, Custom Reptile Habitats, and Zen Habitats.

Some of the major companies in the reptile supplies business are Exo Terra, T-Rex Products, Zilla, and Zoo Med. They develop and sell a variety of products to build and maintain healthy reptile habitats. They sell terrariums of

People can use fish tanks for pet reptiles, but vivariums with secure front doors can make it easier to care for them.

all shapes and sizes and the bedding mixes required by many different reptile species. Their product lines include specialized heaters, lamps, and bulbs to address the temperature and light needs of reptiles, as well as gauges to measure temperature and humidity levels in the tanks. They sell artificial plants and branches, basking rocks, hideouts, and other decor designed to provide captive reptiles with exercise and entertainment. Finally, these companies sell a number of specially formulated reptile foods for different species in powder, pellet, and canned form, as well as vitamins and supplements needed for healthy reptiles.

COSTS

The prices of reptiles vary greatly depending on the species and its rarity, size, and morphs. Common reptile species in their natural coloring are the most affordable. Reptiles that have been bred to have flashier colors than their natural color can cost more. Depending on the type, size, and morph, a snake can cost between $15 and more than $1,000. A corn snake may cost between $40 and $120 and a ball python between $40 and $1,500.[4] A gecko will cost about $20 to $40 at a pet store.[5] Bearded dragons cost between about $40 and $100 at large pet stores or breeders.[6] Turtles range in price from about $10 to $100.[7] Typically, adopting a reptile from a rescue will cost less than buying one from a breeder.

People should be prepared to spend a lot of money on the right equipment and food. Often, the cost of enclosures and supplies is much more expensive than the reptile itself. Owners may need to purchase larger enclosures as the reptile grows. Terrarium prices depend on the size and type. Specially designed wooden enclosures can be $400 and up.[8] Most reptile enclosures require heating and lighting lamps, and the special bulbs need to be replaced every six to 12 months.[9]

For beginners, a starter kit is a simple way to purchase the products needed to build a healthy reptile habitat, and it typically includes a terrarium, bedding, heat and light sources, humidity and temperature gauges, and decor. A crested gecko starter kit sells for about $150 at large pet stores.[10] A leopard gecko kit goes for approximately $180.[11] A bearded dragon starter kit is closer to $350.[12] A snake starter kit is about $200 and up, depending on the size of the snake.[13] An aquatic turtle aquarium kit is about $270.[14]

REPTILE DIY

Reptile owners can save money with do-it-yourself reptile supplies. Owners can make enclosures for both indoor reptiles and outdoor tortoises following directions found in care books, on websites, and on YouTube. Many printed and online care guides include directions for DIY substrate using common ingredients such as organic topsoil and reptile-safe fine sand. Owners can decorate the enclosures with inexpensive items found around the house, such as paper, cardboard boxes and tubes, baskets, rocks, and empty containers.

Food is another ongoing expense. Many reptiles need fresh plants and vegetables daily. What is not eaten must be thrown out at the end of the day and replaced with fresh food the next day. Other reptiles must be fed live insects or frozen animals often. The regular purchase of

Most major pet stores sell frozen feeder animals such as mice for pet reptiles.

live feeder mice, rats, chicks, or rabbits for large snakes is especially costly. As with all pets, reptile owners should factor in the cost of regular veterinary care over the lifetime of the pet.

REPTILE COMMUNITY

A number of international, professional, nonprofit, and independent organizations have formed to support reptile enthusiasts. Some of these organizations publish journals and magazines and maintain blogs and social media pages with a wealth of advice for reptile owners and current research on reptiles in the wild and in captivity. In addition, there are many websites devoted to pet reptiles, the best of which feature science-based guidelines and advice.

The US Association of Reptile Keepers is a nonprofit organization that advocates for responsible private ownership and trade of reptiles. It educates people on good management practices and conservation. It holds its

Veterinarians use resources by the ARAV to learn how to better treat their patients.

members to the Keeper's Code of Ethics, which promotes ethical standards in the keeping, care, breeding, and sale of reptiles and amphibians.

The Association of Reptile and Amphibian Veterinarians (ARAV) is a veterinary organization that promotes the conservation and humane treatment of all reptile and amphibian species through education, medicine, and habitat preservation. The organization publishes the latest research on reptile medicine, care, and conservation in the *Journal of Herpetological Medicine and Surgery* and the monthly electronic newsletter *Herp Blerp*. The organization's website also includes a Find A Vet tool to connect reptile and amphibian pet owners to the best veterinarians for their needs.

The Society for the Study of Amphibians and Reptiles is the largest international nonprofit society devoted to herpetology. It was founded in 1958 to advance the research and conservation of amphibians and reptiles and to educate the public. The organization publishes two journals: the *Journal of Herpetology* and *Herpetological Review*. The *Journal of Herpetology* publishes current research from around the world on the biology of reptiles and amphibians. *The Herpetological Review* publishes research articles, book reviews, news from herpetological societies, and letters from readers. The organization also hosts meetings and other activities and provides

Some herpetological societies travel to schools and teach students about reptiles.

awards and scholarships for educators and students of herpetology.

Many states have one or more herpetological societies. Members of these nonprofit organizations educate the public about reptiles and promote proper care of captive reptiles and conservation of wild reptiles. The societies host meetings, events, and activities, such as educational programs at schools and libraries, field trips, and fundraisers.

Two prominent magazines for reptile hobbyists are *Reptiles Magazine* and *Practical Reptile Keeping*. *Reptiles Magazine* also maintains a website with current news and information and care sheets for many reptile species. *Practical Reptile Keeping* is a monthly magazine published in the United Kingdom. Each issue provides health-care advice, product information, and the latest developments in the reptile world.

Websites that provide science-based information on the care and keeping of reptiles include ReptiFiles, the Reptile Networks, and Behavior Education. The owner and author of the ReptiFiles website is professional reptile husbandry specialist and consultant Mariah Healey. The site includes an extensive database of reptile care guides, a blog, and links to reptile stores, products, veterinarians, and more. The Reptile Networks website is maintained by longtime reptile keeper and published author Pete Hawkins. The site includes evidence-based blog posts and articles on reptile care.

Lori Torrini, an animal trainer and behaviorist, runs the Behavior Education website. Behavior Education focuses on using animal behavior science to improve the quality of life of captive animals and educate their owners. Torrini works with all species but has focused her work on snakes since 2017. The site includes articles, videos, and links on the training, behavior, and welfare of captive animals.

Torrini also maintains a YouTube channel with content about animal training, behavior, enrichment, and welfare. Many of the videos focus on training snakes and their owners to allow the snakes to have choices and control over their own care and interaction with their owners. An example is choice-based handling. This involves reading the snake's behavior and body language to understand whether it is saying "yes" or "no" to being handled. That allows the snake to communicate its wishes and participate in its level of interaction. According to Torrini, this can lead to a trusting relationship between the snake and its owner and safe, fear free handling. Torrini also educates owners about ways to keep snakes mentally healthy through enrichment. Other evidence-based reptile channels on YouTube include Reptiles and Research, JTB Reptiles, Herp HQ, ReptiFiles, and more.

TRADE SHOWS

The North American Reptile Breeders Conference & Trade Shows takes place four times a year in different US cities. Reptile enthusiasts and the general public come together to get up close and personal with reptiles and amphibians. Top breeders from around the world bring their best captive-bred animals for sale. Vendors bring reptile enclosures, supplies, and food for sale. Inspectors move around the convention checking on the health and welfare of the animals being exhibited.

CHAPTER 6

LAWS AND REGULATIONS

The trade of wild and captive reptiles is governed by state, federal, and international laws and regulations. In addition, cities and property owners may restrict the ability to keep some reptiles in captivity. These laws are designed to protect reptiles both in captivity and in the wild. Another focus of the laws is to protect ecosystems from non-native reptiles that might escape or be abandoned after being acquired as pets. In addition, laws and regulations help protect owners and others from reptiles that might cause harm. These laws are constantly changing to address changes in reptile populations and their habitats, so people looking to purchase a reptile should always check the most recent laws before doing so.

It's the owner's responsibility to know whether it is legal to own a specific reptile or whether a license is needed. A buyer should start with international and

US Fish and Wildlife Service officers confiscate smuggled reptiles, including ploughshare tortoises, a critically endangered species.

federal laws to see which reptiles are protected from trade and ownership. Next, they can check state laws for reptiles that are banned or regulated or that require a special permit. Finally, buyers should always check local city laws as well as landlord rules before acquiring a reptile pet.

INTERNATIONAL LAWS

International laws govern which reptiles can be caught in the wild and traded across countries. The Convention on International Trade in Endangered Species of Wild Fauna and Flora (CITES) is the primary piece of international law. CITES is a treaty that regulates the trade of species that

The Chinese crocodile lizard is one endangered reptile whose trade is limited by CITES.

are vulnerable or threatened with extinction. The United States joined CITES in 1975, and since then nearly every country in the world has become a member of CITES.

Approximately 38,000 species of animals are covered by CITES.[1] However, few reptiles are protected. A study found that between 2000 and 2019, nearly 4,000 reptile species were part of the pet trade, most of which was online trade. Of those, only 9 percent were regulated under CITES, even though many traded reptile species are threatened or endangered.[2]

The International Union for Conservation of Nature (IUCN) is an international organization that promotes the conservation of wildlife, though it does not have the power to make laws to protect species. Its Red List of Threatened Species highlights plant and animal species that are threatened with extinction. A 15-year global study of reptiles published in 2022 found that 21 percent of the wild reptile species it assessed are facing extinction.[3] The organization reported that reptile species were decreasing globally, including snakes, skinks, iguanas, chameleons, and geckos. Many of these species are part of the reptile pet trade.

Some of the threatened reptile species that are commonly captured in the wild for the pet trade include the Parson's chameleon, the Indo-Chinese forest lizard, and many geckos, such as the tokay geckos of South

Many people work to protect reptiles, such as the yellow-headed water monitor, from being smuggled.

and Southeast Asia. If a reptile is not listed under CITES or another law, its trade is legal. Some researchers recommend that the law be changed to work the other way around. They would like CITES to generate a list of species that can be legally traded, with trade banned for all species not on the list.

US FEDERAL LAWS

The United States has signed on to various international treaties and passed federal laws and regulations to protect wild plants and animals and their habitats. The most important of these laws is the Endangered Species Act (ESA). Passed in 1973, the ESA sets protections for wildlife that are listed as threatened or endangered and creates plans for the recovery of these species. The ESA defines endangered species as any species that is in danger of disappearing from all or a significant portion of its range. A threatened species is one that is likely to become endangered in the foreseeable future.

NO TINY TURTLES

In the United States, it is illegal to sell, buy, or own turtles with shells less than four inches (10 cm) in length.[7] That's about the size of a deck of cards. Small turtles commonly carry bacteria dangerous to humans called salmonella. One person died in a 2021 salmonella outbreak linked to small turtles. The federal ban of small turtles has been in effect since 1975. Despite that, small turtles are sometimes illegally sold in souvenir shops and at roadside stands.

More than 2,200 species are on the ESA's list of threatened or endangered species.[4] Of those, 50 are reptiles.[5] The ESA makes it illegal to harm or kill species on its protected list. It's also illegal to import, export, or possess these species. Anyone found in possession of a listed species faces fines from $500 to $50,000 and may be arrested.[6] The ESA also protects the habitats of listed wildlife from destruction. According to the World Wildlife Fund, the ESA is very effective, and almost all species protected by the ESA have avoided extinction.

Another important piece of federal legislation is the Lacey Act. The Lacey Act makes it a crime to take, possess, transport, or sell wildlife, fish, and plants that are protected by other federal, state, or international laws. In other words, it helps protect against the illegal trade and trafficking of wildlife. First enacted in 1900, it is the oldest national wildlife protection law in the United States that is still in force. Anyone who violates the law is subject to up to $20,000 in fines and five years in prison.[8]

An additional focus of the Lacey Act is to protect the United States from the introduction of wildlife that may become invasive or otherwise harmful. The act labels these animals "injurious."[9] The act prohibits bringing such species into the country. Prohibiting the introduction of injurious wildlife protects native species, natural resources, agriculture, and human health. In 2015, the Lacey Act listed ten species of reptiles as injurious, including the brown tree snake, four species of anacondas, and five species of pythons, including the Burmese python.[10] Under the Lacey Act, it is illegal to import injurious wildlife into the country. Amendments to the Lacey Act proposed in 2021 would extend protections, including making

Because of how large they can grow, Burmese pythons can be dangerous to their owners and to others if they escape.

LACEY ACT AMENDMENTS

When changes are proposed to federal regulations, the public is allowed to comment before the changes are finalized. In 2021, the proposed amendments to the Lacey Act generated comments from concerned reptile breeders and owners. They worried that reptile species currently kept as pets in the United States might be put on the injurious list. That would prevent breeders and suppliers from shipping reptiles to other states, which would hurt their business. Reptile owners expressed concern that they wouldn't be able to take pet reptiles with them if they moved across state lines or needed to seek veterinary care in another state. As a result, that portion of the amendment was removed from the bill.

it illegal to transport injurious wildlife across state borders. It also would authorize the US Department of the Interior to add species to the Lacey Act list on an emergency basis.

STATE LAWS

Laws regarding captive reptiles vary greatly from state to state. Some places have no regulations. Others require permits to own certain animals, and some prohibit certain species altogether.

State regulations also may require that exotic pets such as reptiles be well cared for and kept in clean and proper enclosures. The reptiles most likely to be the subject of state laws are snakes. Most states ban people from breeding, selling, or owning venomous snakes, including rattlesnakes, copperheads, and water moccasins, or require special permits to do so.

States rarely forbid people or require permits to breed, trade, or own nonvenomous snakes and other reptiles that are commonly kept as pets, such as corn snakes, rosy boas, and ball pythons. In general, states don't consider these species a threat to people or the environment. There are some exceptions, though. For example, the state of Georgia restricts the possession of many nonvenomous snakes. Hawaii bans all pet snakes. States that regulate or ban nonvenomous reptiles generally do so to protect local habitats and species from non-native species.

Before acquiring a reptile pet, buyers should always check their state and city laws. A good place to start is a state's department of natural resources or local wildlife agency. In addition, reptile owners should know that it is typically illegal to release a reptile that is not native to that state.

SNAKE-FREE HAWAII

Unlike most tropical islands, Hawaii has no native snakes. The only snakes currently on the Hawaiian Islands are those that have been released or escaped. These non-native snakes can have devastating effects on the native plants and animals of Hawaii. For this reason, it is illegal to own a pet snake of any kind in Hawaii. Bringing snakes to Hawaii is a felony punishable by fines of up to $200,000 and three years in prison.[11]

CHAPTER 7

REPTILE DEBATES

Reptiles are becoming increasingly popular as pets, but the reptile pet trade is not without its controversies. A major concern is the sustainability of wild populations of reptiles. Reptile numbers are declining worldwide, and part of the problem is the capture of wild reptiles for the pet trade. Another concern is the number of reptile pets that escape or are released into the wild. These discarded pets can disrupt habitats in which they are not native. Finally, there are the ethical concerns of keeping undomesticated animals as pets. It can be difficult to provide a wild animal with a good quality of life in an enclosure.

Hognose snakes are among the many snakes available from breeders.

WILDLIFE TRAFFICKING

Thousands of reptile species are threatened by a global pet trade that is poorly regulated. That lack of regulation means that vulnerable populations of reptiles, and even ones that are illegal to capture, are still traded. The illegal trade of animals is known as wildlife trafficking.

Many reptile collectors like to own rare and unusual reptiles. As a result, some reptile suppliers seek out threatened species that have declining numbers in

Smuggled animals are often kept in inhumane conditions during transport.

the wild. Others look for members of newly discovered reptile species that have yet to receive protections. It is not uncommon for reptile sellers to claim that wild-caught reptiles were bred in captivity in order to get around laws against their trade.

A study published in 2020 found that globally, approximately 90 percent of traded reptile species are captured from the wild, including endangered and protected species.[1] For example, boa constrictors are so popular as pets that some subspecies of the snake have become endangered in the wild and are protected. Chameleons also make popular pets, but wild populations are in trouble. Protected species of chameleons in Madagascar continue to be illegally collected for the pet trade. Other endangered lizards that are commonly captured and traded include tokay geckos, the Indo-Chinese forest lizard, and the electric blue day gecko. Turtles and tortoises threatened by the illegal pet trade include the pancake turtle of Africa, the Hermann's tortoise of southern Europe, and the Indian star tortoise.

Many conservationists and people who care about reptiles are committed to protecting them from the illegal wildlife trade. In 2022, CITES added 127 reptile species to the list of animals regulated or banned from trade.[2] That is one of the biggest listing increases since the treaty began in 1975.

Better regulation of the global trade in reptiles, stronger laws, and public education campaigns may help protect reptiles around the world. In addition, reptile owners can help greatly by reducing the demand for rare and wild reptiles. First, people should not capture a wild reptile and keep it as a pet. Wild-caught reptiles are always better off in their natural habitat, since adapting to captivity can cause them stress. Second, people should not purchase a reptile that is on a list of threatened or protected species. And finally, to discourage wildlife trafficking, buyers should look for animals that were bred and born in captivity.

Besides helping conserve wild populations, reptiles bred and born in captivity will typically be healthier and easier to interact with. Species that are commonly bred in captivity include bearded dragons, crested and leopard geckos, northern blue-tongued skinks, and ball pythons. Additionally, people can adopt a reptile from a rescue, providing a new home to an animal whose original owner can no longer care for it. The goal is eventually for all reptiles sold to be captive bred.

RELEASING REPTILES

Every year, reptile owners in the United States release their non-native pets into the wild, even when it is illegal to do so. Some owners may find themselves no longer

REPTILE SPOTLIGHT

CRESTED GECKO

Crested geckos are rare in the wild, and the species was thought to be extinct until it was rediscovered in New Caledonia in the 1990s. New Caledonia is a group of islands between Fiji and Australia. Crested geckos live in the trees and vines of these tropical rain forest islands. They are active at night, and their big eyes have exceptional night vision. The species is protected in the wild, but successful captive breeding programs have resulted in many crested geckos entering the reptile pet trade.

Crested geckos are fairly small lizards, about eight inches (20 cm) long. They naturally occur in colors from cream to dark brown but have been bred to have a variety of colors and patterns. Their most striking pattern is a row of pointed scales that runs from above each eye and down the back. These spikes give the big-eyed lizard the appearance of eyelashes.

Crested geckos are wonderful climbers. They have wide toes with brush-like hooks on the pads. This enables them to climb smooth surfaces like glass and hang upside down from ceilings. They can live for 15 to 20 years or more in captivity when cared for properly.[3]

Brown anoles, which are native to the Caribbean, have become invasive in Hawaii.

able to care for their pet. They may have acquired the reptile without realizing how much care and expense was involved or how long the reptile was going to live. Others may be surprised at how large or aggressive their pet has become. For a few owners, the novelty of owning a reptile simply wears off.

Some owners may think that their reptile will be fine outside, but most abandoned reptiles suffer. Reptiles from warmer climates may die of cold if released in a cooler climate. Because most captive reptiles lack survival skills, they can also die of starvation or be killed by predators. Sometimes escaped or released reptile pets survive and even thrive. They might breed and establish growing populations in their new home. This is good news for the released reptile but bad news for the environment. Non-native reptiles compete with native species for food and territory. They may prey on native species. In addition, pet reptiles may carry germs and diseases into wild populations. When non-native species take hold, native species decline, and ecosystems are disrupted.

Chameleons, for example, are not native to the United States, but populations of former pet chameleons are found in several states. Veiled chameleons from Yemen and Saudi Arabia now live in Florida and Hawaii, where they prey on native species of insects and birds. Hawaii also is home to Jackson's chameleons from East Africa. In 1972, a few dozen escaped or were released from a pet store there, and the species has been spreading across the islands ever since. Released iguanas have become pests in Florida, Hawaii, and other warm places where they have no natural predators. These non-native lizards eat native plant and animal species and even damage buildings by burrowing underneath them.

Corn snakes are common snake pets that are native to the eastern and southeastern United States. Now populations of corn snakes are found outside their natural range, including in Europe, the Caribbean, and Hawaii, which has no native snakes. The snakes reached these places as escaped or released pets.

REPTILE SANCTUARY

The Reptile Rescue Center of Little Rock, Arkansas, has been helping reptiles since 2009. Its mission is threefold: rescue, rehabilitation, and education. The center takes in reptiles from across the country that have been surrendered, injured, abused, or neglected. It provides veterinary care and deals with behavioral issues so that each reptile can be a good pet for a new owner. The center also educates the public about owners' responsibilities to provide proper care for reptiles and about conservation of wild reptiles. The center offers reptiles for adoption after carefully screening and educating new owners.

Burmese pythons are threatened in many areas of their natural range, but members of this species released by owners have become devastating pests elsewhere. These long snakes have invaded parts of Florida, including the Everglades. They are excellent hunters that are eating their way through the birds and mammals native to Florida. Burmese pythons even prey

The Florida Fish and Wildlife Conservation Commission (FWC) allows people to capture and humanely kill Burmese pythons on private and FWC-owned lands without a license or limit. This is to try to reduce the numbers.

on alligators. The populations of native Florida mammals have declined sharply since the pythons became established. Florida has one of the world's most serious invasive species problems in the world due to the reptile pet trade.

If people can no longer care for their reptiles, reptile rescue centers throughout the United States can take in these reptiles. Some rescue centers also care for sick and injured reptiles. The goals of these centers are to keep the reptiles healthy and find new homes for them.

Some reptile centers also teach owners how to properly care for their pets. Rescue center volunteers can help care for animals or provide foster homes until a permanent home is found.

EXOTIC PETS

Domesticated animals, such as dogs and cats, have evolved traits over thousands of years that have improved their ability to live alongside humans in homes. Undomesticated animals like reptiles, on the other hand, still have their natural traits that allow them to thrive in the wild. Undomesticated animals, or exotic pets, present more challenges for pet owners.

Some reptile owners research the best ways to care for their animals and provide them with a good environment to live in. However, a large number of reptile owners do not know how to care for them. According to biologists and veterinarians writing in the British

A HARD FIRST YEAR

Many reptiles face a hard journey on the way to a home as a pet. An estimated 90 percent of reptiles caught in the wild to be sold as pets die within their first year of captivity.[4] This is due to the trauma of capture, inhumane treatment during shipment, and inadequate care by the new owner. Some reptile enthusiasts work to educate potential buyers about laws and conservation to help reduce the interest in wild-caught reptiles.

veterinary journal *In Practice*, most reptiles in captivity, unlike dogs and cats, will be restricted to small enclosures maintained by owners who don't adequately meet their needs. Exotic species veterinarian Bairbre O'Malley noted that many owners buy reptiles without a basic knowledge of what their new pets need. New reptile owners often rely on information provided by the pet store, which she said is usually not enough to properly care for the animals. An estimated 70 percent of pet reptile illnesses are caused by poor care. As much as 75 percent of reptiles die during their first year in a home.[5]

Exotic animal specialists note that with the right information, owners can provide pet reptiles with proper care and a healthy life. They recommend improving pet keeper education and increasing access to specialist veterinary care.

CHAPTER 8

REPTILE OWNERSHIP

Reptiles come with unique challenges that can make it difficult for them to thrive in captivity. But it is possible, with effort and knowledge, to properly look after many kinds of reptiles. Recent research and trends in care are helping improve the well-being of captive reptiles. Reptiles can make good pets for knowledgeable and dedicated owners.

BENEFITS OF PET REPTILES

Reptiles are a good fit for many households because they are relatively quiet and odorless. They spend most of their time in a vivarium and so are not free to roam the house where they could make a mess. Many don't require training for behavioral issues. In addition, reptiles, unlike pets with fur, pose almost no risk of allergy to owners.

Chinese water dragons require a fair amount of care because they need a very hot, humid habitat. But owners enjoy the friendly nature of these reptiles.

EMOTIONAL SUPPORT REPTILES

If a reptile helps an owner feel calmer and more capable than they do without the pet, it may be possible to register it as an emotional support animal. Most emotional support animals are dogs, but many other pets can qualify, including reptiles. Many people find that their reptiles, such as snakes, create a soothing presence that helps lessen anxiety. Registering an emotional support animal requires documentation from a mental health professional that the animal is helpful for the owner who is coping with a mental health condition. Being an emotional support animal does not grant the animal permission to go to public places such as restaurants or stores, but it does mean that landlords can't refuse to allow the animal to live on the premises.

Allergies to reptiles are extremely rare.

Reptiles are not only relatively clean and allergy-free but are also entertaining pets to own and observe because they are very different from traditional pets. They may climb, slither, jump, or walk around their enclosures. At times a reptile pet may be basking on a rock under a warm lamp, and at other times it may be tucked under a plant for shade and quiet time. Some reptiles enjoy being petted and held.

Reptile pets can be an important part of public education programs, helping dispel myths about them. Many people are afraid of snakes and other reptiles. People who visit homes with pet reptiles may come to learn that the animals are generally calm. Their skin feels smooth, almost like velvet. Pet reptiles can help the public be less fearful of reptiles, which could lead to more public support for reptile conservation programs. As one owner of a pet turtle named Mr. Pokey reflected, "I cannot deny that I love a turtle. In loving this one, I have come to care about all turtles, and even to imagine that I am on the road to caring about all living creatures."[1]

All pets provide comfort and companionship, and that includes reptiles. Reptiles and other pets contribute to their owners' well-being in a number of ways, including improving mood, reducing loneliness, and providing a sense of purpose. A study in 2021 found evidence that the emotional bond owners feel for their reptile pets is similar to the attachments for pet cats and dogs.

The feeling may be mutual. Whether reptiles experience complex emotions is a relatively new field of science, but research is offering some fascinating insights into the interior lives of reptiles. A 2019 review of scientific literature found 37 articles that suggested that reptiles are capable of a range of emotions, including anxiety, stress, distress, excitement, fear, frustration, pain, and suffering.[2]

A few studies offer evidence that reptiles feel pleasure. Do reptiles experience love? Some reptile owners insist that their pets known them and like them. Others report that some lizards and tortoises especially enjoy being stroked and close their eyes in pleasure. According to Dr. Sharman Hoppes, clinical professor at the Texas

A&M College of Veterinary Medicine & Biomedical Sciences, some reptiles do seem to recognize their owners and enjoy their company. "I don't know if it is love," says Dr. Hoppes, "but lizards and tortoises appear to like some people more than others."[3] Recognizing that reptiles are animals with emotions could help improve the treatment of reptiles in captivity and improve their lives.

TRENDS IN REPTILE CARE

Due to a lack of understanding, myths about the care of reptiles have taken hold, such as the belief that large enclosures are stressful for reptiles and that these sedentary creatures don't need exercise or stimulation. Research leading to a better understanding of reptiles and their natural behaviors is changing the way people care for their reptile pets. Reptile experts now recommend that reptiles in captivity be provided opportunities to exercise, explore, and interact with their owners on their own terms.

The Behavior Education website says, "We work with animals to teach cooperative behaviors so that they may voluntarily participate in their own care and become socialized family members."[4] Since 2017, much of the organization's work has focused on snakes. By learning a pet snake's body language, an owner knows whether it is relaxed or stressed. For example, if a snake is stretched out comfortably in the open, alert but calmly breathing, and moving slowly and fluidly, it is likely relaxed. This is how a snake should behave the majority of the time. This is a good time to interact with the snake.

On the other hand, if the snake is hiding, has a tight, tense body that is coiled or wrapped tightly, or is moving with twitchy, jerky movements, it is becoming stressed. The snake needs quiet time to relax before handling. If a snake is in a stressed state much of the time, the owner needs to address its care needs. Understanding a reptile's

Certain types of reptiles can be exercised on a harness and leash.

behavior and responding in a way that addresses its needs gives the animal some control over its own care, which is an important aspect of good captive animal care.

Another trend in captive reptile care is the emphasis on providing the animals with an active and engaging environment. Reptiles cared for by humans no longer need to work for their survival, so they have energy to burn. Without an outlet for that energy, captive reptiles can become stressed. They may rub their noses on objects, move constantly and restlessly around their enclosures, and even hurt themselves.

Owners can provide their reptiles with mental and physical stimulation. A study in 1996 showed that providing a captive turtle with objects such as balls, sticks, and hoses led to a decrease in self-harm. Another study of Komodo dragons showed that providing enrichment items tripled their activity levels. Enrichment items include plants, rocks, branches, and hideouts. These items encourage reptiles to dig, climb, and explore. Even small periodic changes such as rearranging decor in the enclosure can encourage more exploration and activity. Some companies have begun producing toys for reptiles specifically designed to promote their natural foraging instincts. For example, puzzle feeders for snakes encourage them to spend more time searching for their food, like they would in the wild.

SOCIAL MEDIA

Social media has popularized the keeping of exotic pets, including reptiles. Images, videos, and descriptions of interesting reptiles get people excited about owning one of their own. The rise of social media has had both advantages and disadvantages for reptiles and their keepers.

Social media provides an easy way for reptile sellers and buyers to connect. Online trade has become a major avenue for global reptile sales. It also provides an easy way for wild reptile traffickers and other unethical reptile suppliers to market their animals. People can now purchase a wild-caught reptile on social platforms such as Facebook Marketplace and from individuals with just the click of a button. Such a quick and easy process can result in an impulsive purchase without the proper research to prepare a buyer for owning a reptile and ensuring

BOOKS WITH BEARDED DRAGONS

Bearded dragons can be found in the wild, in homes, and now in school libraries. Bearded dragons make good library pets because they're quiet, safe, and low energy. Librarians report that the friendly but calm reptiles encourage reading. Students come into libraries daily to hang out with the resident bearded dragon and leave with a book. Even reluctant readers are eager to read to a lizard. It's a win-win for reptiles and reading.

It's important that owners learn their species' body language so they know how to tell if it is stressed by handling.

that it is a captive-bred animal from a reputable source. In addition, much misinformation about the care and keeping of reptiles can be spread on social media.

On the other hand, social media and mobile apps can be important tools for reptile education, information, and outreach. Facebook and other online social networking services provide an opportunity for reptile enthusiasts to connect with others and share advice, information, and support.

A number of reputable social media groups focus on reptile rescue and rehoming. Many are run by nonprofit organizations around the world. Others are dedicated to connecting buyers and sellers. Reptile enthusiasts can purchase reptiles as well as food and supplies on these and other sites and read reviews from buyers.

There are also mobile apps, many of which are free, devoted to the education, care, and enjoyment of reptiles. Reptile Books is an app dedicated to educating the public about reptiles. The mobile app SnakeKeeper provides a way for snake owners to track their snake's weight and length as well as its feeding and shedding schedules. This app can help owners easily identify sudden changes that could indicate a health issue.

Caring for reptile pets can be a rewarding and enriching experience for owners. It can also be helpful for improving the treatment and public perception of all reptiles. When owners choose an animal wisely and care for it properly, they can enjoy the comfort and companionship of their reptile pet for many years.

REPTILE AWARENESS DAY

Reptile Awareness Day takes place every year on October 21. It's a day for reptile enthusiasts to celebrate their pets. It's also a day to help improve the reputation of snakes and other reptiles, educate the public on their roles in habitats around the world, and promote conservation efforts. The first Reptile Awareness Day may date back to 1966, when the first Endangered Species Act was passed. Reptile lovers can support the day on social media using the hashtag #ReptileAwarenessDay.

ESSENTIAL FACTS

OWNING A REPTILE

Reptiles kept as pets include snakes, lizards, turtles, and tortoises. There are more than 10,000 known species of reptiles. In the United States in 2021 and 2022, 5.7 million homes kept at least one reptile as a pet.

DIET: Snakes are carnivores. Lizards, turtles, and tortoises can be insectivores, herbivores, or carnivores.

SPACE: Reptiles in captivity live in enclosures with bedding, light, heat sources, and humidity that mimic their natural environment as closely as possible. The cage needs enough space to have a warm and cool side. The bigger the cage, the better.

ROUTINE CARE: Care varies by species, but it includes feeding regularly, cleaning the cage, and monitoring the temperatures and humidity levels. Reptiles should see the veterinarian at least once a year.

ENRICHMENT: Owners should regularly move and change hiding places and decorations. They can also train their reptiles to perform behaviors, let them explore a safe space out of their tanks, and even take some outside on a harness and leash.

KEY SPECIES

- Corn snakes are midsize, active snakes that like to climb and explore.
- Ball pythons are popular pets that are named for their habit of curling into a tight ball.
- The crested gecko lives mainly in the trees and is a popular pet gecko.
- Bearded dragons are generally calm and friendly, but they spread a beard-like flap of skin when disturbed.
- Leopard geckos are small lizards with brown or black spots to blend into their desert surroundings in the wild. They live primarily on the ground.
- Box turtles are terrestrial. Native to the United States, they are one of the less challenging species of turtles to keep.
- Russian tortoises need large enclosures, preferably outdoors, and can live up to 50 years.

GLOSSARY

amendment
A formal addition or change to a document.

ectotherm
An animal that regulates its body temperature through external sources, such as sunlight and shade.

enrichment
The act or process of making life richer by adding or increasing desirable things.

foraging
Searching for food.

herpetology
The study of reptiles and amphibians.

husbandry
The care and management of captive animals.

hygrometer
An instrument for measuring humidity in the air or in confined spaces.

insectivore
An animal that eats insects for food.

keratin
A type of protein that makes up features such as hair, skin, and nails.

morph

A skin color or pattern different than what the same animals would have in nature and that people have developed by breeding captive animals.

scute

A large, bony plate; in turtles specifically, a piece that makes up the carapace.

substrate

The surface on which organisms live, such as sand or soil.

territorial

Concerned with ownership or defense of a particular area.

vertebrate

An animal with a spinal column and a brain that is part of its nervous system.

vivarium

An enclosed container in which a small animal such as a reptile is kept.

ADDITIONAL RESOURCES

SELECTED BIBLIOGRAPHY

Amelia, Peter. "Puzzle Feeding for Snakes." *IAABC Journal*, n.d., iaabcjournal.org. Accessed 23 Nov. 2022.

"Healthy Pets, Healthy People: Reptiles and Amphibians." *Centers for Disease Control and Prevention*, 28 Feb. 2022, cdc.gov. Accessed 31 Oct. 2022.

Mattison, Chris. *Snakes and Other Reptiles and Amphibians*. DK, 2014.

FURTHER READINGS

de Vosjoli, Philippe, Robert Mailloux, Susan Donoghue, et al. *Bearded Dragon Manual*. Fox Chapel, 2022.

Edwards, Sue Bradford. *The Evolution of Reptiles*. Abdo, 2019.

Hale, K. A. *Essential Reptiles*. Abdo, 2022.

ONLINE RESOURCES

Booklinks
NONFICTION NETWORK
FREE! ONLINE NONFICTION RESOURCES

To learn more about pet reptiles, please visit **abdobooklinks.com** or scan this QR code. These links are routinely monitored and updated to provide the most current information available.

MORE INFORMATION

For more information on this subject, contact or visit the following organizations:

American Society of Ichthyologists and Herpetologists (ASIH)

810 E. 10th St.
Lawrence, KS 66044
asih@allenpress.com
asih.org

The ASIH works to increase scientific knowledge about fish, reptiles, and amphibians and to get that information to the public.

Association of Reptile and Amphibian Veterinarians (ARAV)

PO Box 1868
Mt. Juliet, TN 37121
info@arav.org
arav.org

The ARAV educates veterinarians about new discoveries in veterinary care for reptiles and amphibians. It also provides information for reptile owners as well as a tool to help owners find vets who specialize in reptiles.

San Diego Zoo Wildlife Alliance: Reptiles

2920 Zoo Dr.
San Diego, CA 92101
animals.sandiegozoo.org/animals/reptiles

The San Diego Zoo Wildlife Alliance has information about reptiles as a group. It also has information about a variety of reptile species, from size and diet to behavior.

SOURCE NOTES

CHAPTER 1. A NEW PET

1. Tom Fish. "How Long Do Lizards Live? Reptile Lifespan Explained." *Newsweek*, 11 Mar. 2022, newsweek.com. Accessed 8 Feb. 2023.

2. *Bearded Dragon (*Pogona vitticeps*)*. ReptiFiles, 2020. reptifiles.com. Accessed 8 Feb. 2023.

3. *Bearded Dragon (*Pogona vitticeps*)*.

4. "Pet Industry Market Size, Trends & Ownership Statistics." *American Pet Products Association*, n.d., americanpetproducts.org. Accessed 8 Feb. 2023.

5. "A Report on Reptile Pet Ownership in the United States." *Reptiles Cove*, n.d., reptilescove.com. Accessed 8 Feb. 2023.

6. Mariah Healey. "Bearded Dragon Care Guide." *ReptiFiles*, 2 July 2015, reptifiles.com. Accessed 8 Feb. 2023.

CHAPTER 2. NATURAL HISTORY OF REPTILES

1. "Home Page." *Reptile Database*, n.d., reptile-database.reptarium.cz. Accessed 8 Feb. 2023.

2. "*Spinosaurus*." *Natural History Museum*, n.d., nhm.ac.uk. Accessed 8 Feb. 2023.

3. George R. Zug and Herndon G. Dowling. "Reptile." *Encyclopedia Britannica*, 22 Sept. 2022, britannica.com. Accessed 8 Feb. 2023.

4. Zug and Dowling, "Reptile."

5. "Serpentes." *ScienceDirect*, n.d., sciencedirect.com. Accessed 8 Feb. 2023.

6. Mark O'Shea. *The Book of Snakes: A Life-Size Guide to Six Hundred Species from around the World*. University of Chicago, 2018. Excerpt (Barnes & Noble), n.d., barnesandnoble.com.

7. "Python Temple." *Lonely Planet*, n.d., lonelyplanet.com. Accessed 8 Feb. 2023.

8. "Serpentes."

9. Zug and Dowling, "Reptile."

10. George R. Zug. "Turtle." *Encyclopedia Britannica*, 8 Feb. 2023, britannica.com. Accessed 8 Feb. 2023.

11. "Chelonians (Turtles, Tortoises)." *Veterian Key*, 27 Aug. 2016, veteriankey.com. Accessed 8 Feb. 2023.

12. Zug, "Turtle."

13. Mike Corcoran. "The Rise of Reptiles and What It Means for Veterinary Medicine." *PetVet Magazine*, 8 Apr. 2021, petvetmagazine.com. Accessed 8 Feb. 2023.

CHAPTER 3. CHOOSING AND PREPARING FOR REPTILES

1. Tom Fish. "How Long Do Lizards Live? Reptile Lifespan Explained." *Newsweek*, 11 Mar. 2022, newsweek.com. Accessed 8 Feb. 2023.

2. "Selecting a Pet Reptile." *American Veterinary Medical Association*, n.d., avma.org. Accessed 8 Feb. 2023.

3. Bairbre O'Malley. "Reptiles: Husbandry and Common Conditions." *Irish Veterinary Journal*, vol. 60, no. 5, pp. 303–309. 304.

4. O'Malley, "Reptiles," 304–305.

5. Summer Fiori. "Reptiles as Companion Animals." *Writing about Animals*, 1 Jan. 2020, companionanimals.commons.gc.cuny.edu. Accessed 8 Feb. 2023.

CHAPTER 4. CARING FOR REPTILES

1. *Corn Snake (*Pantherophis guttatus*). ReptiFiles*, 2020, reptifiles.com. Accessed 8 Feb. 2023.

2. *Ball Python (*Python regius*). ReptiFiles*, 2020, reptifiles.com. Accessed 8 Feb. 2023.

3. *Corn Snake (*Pantherophis guttatus*).*

4. Mariah Healey. "Rosy Boa Care Sheet." *ReptiFiles*, n.d., reptifiles.com. Accessed 8 Feb. 2023.

5. Mariah Healey. "ReptiFiles® Lizard Care Sheets." *ReptiFiles*, n.d., reptifiles.com. Accessed 8 Feb. 2023.

6. *Eastern Blue Tongue Skink (*Tiliqua scincoides scincoides*). ReptiFiles*, 2020, reptifiles.com. Accessed 8 Feb. 2023.

7. Healey, "ReptiFiles® Lizard Care Sheets."

8. Healey, "ReptiFiles® Lizard Care Sheets."

9. Darren Naish. "Skinks, Skinks, Skinks!" *Scientific American*, 10 Oct. 2014, blogs.scientificamerican.com. Accessed 8 Feb. 2023.

10. Phil Goss. "Blue-Tongue Skink Care Sheet." *Reptiles Magazine*, 10 Apr. 2012, reptilesmagazine.com. Accessed 8 Feb. 2023.

11. Mariah Healey. "Sulcata Tortoise Care Sheet." *ReptiFiles*, n.d., reptifiles.com. Accessed 8 Feb. 2023.

12. Mariah Healey. "Russian Tortoise Care Sheet." *ReptiFiles*, n.d., reptifiles.com. Accessed 8 Feb. 2023.

13. Healey, "Russian Tortoise Care Sheet."

14. Mariah Healey. "Eastern Box Turtle Care Sheet." *ReptiFiles*, n.d., reptifiles.com. Accessed 8 Feb. 2023.

15. Healey, "Russian Tortoise Care Sheet."

16. *Red-Eared Slider (*Trachemys scripta elegans*). ReptiFiles*, 2020, reptifiles.com. Accessed 8 Feb. 2023.

17. "Pet Turtle Tank and Water Maintenance." *BeChewy*, 6 Sept. 2022, be.chewy.com. Accessed 8 Feb. 2023.

SOURCE NOTES CONTINUED

CHAPTER 5. INDUSTRY AND COMMUNITY

1. "US Market for Pet Reptiles in the US Pet Market: Impact of Coronavirus Pandemic." *GlobeNewswire*, 14 May 2020, globenewswire.com. Accessed 8 Feb. 2023.

2. "Breeders in US & Canada." *MorphMarket*, n.d., morphmarket.com. Accessed 8 Feb. 2023.

3. "Home Page." *MorphMarket*, n.d., morphmarket.com. Accessed 8 Feb. 2023.

4. Oliver Jones. "How Much Does a Snake Cost? (2023 Price Guide)." *Pet Keen*, 7 Feb. 2023, petkeen.com. Accessed 8 Feb. 2023.

5. Elizabeth Gray. "How Much Do Leopard Geckos Cost at PetSmart?" *Pet Keen*, 3 Feb. 2023, petkeen.com. Accessed 8 Feb. 2023.

6. Dean Eby. "How Much Does a Bearded Dragon Cost? (2023 Price Guide)." *Pet Keen*, 11 Jan. 2023, petkeen.com. Accessed 8 Feb. 2023.

7. Nicole Cosgrove. "How Much Does a Turtle Cost? (2023 Update)." *Pet Keen*, 6 Jan. 2023, petkeen.com. Accessed 8 Feb. 2023.

8. "Reptile Enclosures." *Zen Habitats*, n.d., zenhabitats.com. Accessed 8 Feb. 2023.

9. "Selecting a Pet Reptile." *American Veterinary Medical Association*, n.d., avma.org. Accessed 8 Feb. 2023.

10. "Exo-Terra Crested Gecko Kit." *Petco*, n.d., petco.com. Accessed 8 Feb. 2023.

11. "Exo Terra Leopard Gecko Starter Kit." *Petco*, n.d., petco.com. Accessed 8 Feb. 2023.

12. "Exo Terra Adult Bearded Dragon Starter Kit." *Petco*, n.d., petco.com. Accessed 8 Feb. 2023.

13. "Zilla Premium Snake Kit, 20 Long." *Petco*, n.d., petco.com. Accessed 8 Feb. 2023.

14. "Zilla Aquatic Turtle Aquarium Kit, 20 Long." *Petco*, n.d., petco.com. Accessed 8 Feb. 2023.

CHAPTER 6. LAWS AND REGULATIONS

1. "CITES: The Convention on International Trade in Endangered Species of Fauna and Flora." *World Wildlife Fund*, n.d., worldwildlife.org. Accessed 8 Feb. 2023.

2. Benjamin M. Marshall, Colin Strine, and Alice C. Hughes. "Thousands of Reptile Species Threatened by Under-Regulated Global Trade." *Nature Communications*, vol. 11, no. 4738, 29 Sept. 2020, nature.com. Accessed 8 Feb. 2023.

3. Neil Cox, et al. "A Global Reptile Assessment Highlights Shared Conservation Needs of Tetrapods." *Nature*, vol. 605, 2022, pp. 285–290, nature.com. Accessed 8 Feb. 2023.

4. "The Endangered Species Act." *Center for Biological Diversity*, n.d., biologicaldiversity.org. Accessed 8 Feb. 2023.

5. "FWS-Listed US Species by Taxonomic Group—Reptiles." *US Fish & Wildlife Service Environmental Conservation Online System*, n.d., ecos.fws.gov. Accessed 8 Feb. 2023.

6. Cynthia F. Hodges. "Brief Summary of the Endangered Species Act (ESA)." *Michigan State University Animal Legal & Historical Center*, 2010, animallaw.info. Accessed 8 Feb. 2023.

7. "Salmonella and Turtle Safety." *US Food & Drug Administration*, 9 Aug. 2022, fda.gov. Accessed 8 Feb. 2023.

8. Cynthia F. Hodges. "Brief Summary of the Lacey Act." *Michigan State University Animal Legal & Historical Center*, 2010, animallaw.info. Accessed 8 Feb. 2023.

9. "S.626 - Lacey Act Amendments of 2021." *Congress.gov*, 9 Mar. 2021, congress.gov. Accessed 8 Feb. 2023.

10. "Summary of Species Currently Listed as Injurious Wildlife under (18 U.S.C. 42) Lacey Act." *US Fish & Wildlife Service*, n.d., fws.gov. Accessed 8 Feb. 2023.

11. Lou Carter. "Snakes That Live in Hawaii (Venomous Sea Snakes & Invasive Species)." *Snakes for Pets*, 15 Dec. 2020, snakesforpets.com. Accessed 8 Feb. 2023.

CHAPTER 7. REPTILE DEBATES

1. Benjamin M. Marshall, Colin Strine, and Alice C. Hughes. "Thousands of Reptile Species Threatened by Under-Regulated Global Trade." *Nature Communications*, vol. 11, no. 4738, 29 Sept. 2020, nature.com. Accessed 8 Feb. 2023.

2. Paige Bennett. "127 Reptiles Added to Global Treaty against Wildlife Trade." *EcoWatch*, 4 Apr. 2022, ecowatch.com. Accessed 8 Feb. 2023.

3. Mariah Healey. "Crested Gecko Care Guide." *ReptiFiles*, n.d., reptifiles.com. Accessed 8 Feb. 2023.

4. James M. Green. "Trade in Wild-Caught Reptiles." *Michigan State University Animal Legal & Historical Center*, 2005, animallaw.info. Accessed 8 Feb. 2023.

5. Alexandre Azevedo, Leonor Guimarães, Joel Ferraz, Martin Whiting, and Manuel Magalhães-Sant'Ana. "Pet Reptiles—Are We Meeting Their Needs?" *Animals*, vol. 11, no. 10, 2021, p. 2964, mdpi.com. Accessed 8 Feb. 2023.

CHAPTER 8. REPTILE OWNERSHIP

1. Kate McReynolds. "Mr. Pokey: A Turtle Diary." *ENCOUNTER: Education for Meaning and Social Justice*, vol. 18, no. 4, winter 2005, p. 9.

2. Helen Lambert, Gemma Carder, and Neil D'Cruze. "Given the Cold Shoulder: A Review of the Scientific Literature for Evidence of Reptile Sentience." *Animals (Basel)*, vol. 9, no. 10, 17 Oct. 2019, p. 821, ncbi.nlm.nih.gov. Accessed 8 Feb. 2023.

3. "Reptile Emotions." *Texas A&M Today*, 18 Aug. 2011, today.tamu.edu. Accessed 8 Feb. 2023.

4. "Home." *Behavior Education, Studies, and Training*, n.d., behavioreducation.org. Accessed 8 Feb. 2023.

INDEX

aggression, 30, 39, 46, 84
apps, 98–99
Asia, 17, 18, 27, 41, 50, 72
Association of Reptile and Amphibian Veterinarians (ARAV), 37–38, 64
Association of Reptile Keepers, US, 63
Australia, 7, 9, 27, 83

Behavior Education, 66, 94
behaviors, 9, 22, 36, 38–39, 46, 56, 66–67, 86, 91, 94–95
breeders, 7, 11, 27, 55–57, 58, 60, 64, 67, 76, 83

carnivores, 18, 23, 35, 45
communication, 17, 67
Convention on International Trade in Endangered Species of Wild Fauna and Flora (CITES), 70–72, 81
costs, 30, 60–62
crocodiles, 14–15, 26

decorations, 7, 43, 59, 61, 96
Department of the Interior, US, 76
dinosaurs, 13, 14
  Microraptor, 14
  Spinosaurus, 14

ectotherms, 5, 11, 15, 41
eggs, 16
Egypt, 26
emotional support, 92
emotions, 93–94
Endangered Species Act (ESA), 73
enrichment, 33, 53, 56, 67, 94, 96
exotic pets, 7, 38, 76, 88–89, 97

Florida, 85–87
food, 8, 16–19, 21, 23, 25–26, 29, 33, 35, 39, 45, 48, 53, 60–61, 67, 85, 96, 99

Georgia, 77

handling, 30, 36–37, 46, 53, 56, 67, 95
Hawaii, 77, 85–86
herbivores, 16, 35, 53
herpetological societies, 64–65
humidity, 6, 8, 10, 33–35, 37, 44–45, 47–49, 51, 56, 59, 61
hygrometers, 8, 35, 56

insectivores, 33, 35
International Union for Conservation of Nature (IUCN), 71
invasive species, 47, 74, 87

Lacey Act, 74–76
life spans, 6, 15, 24, 26, 30, 48–49, 50, 83
light, 6–9, 10, 32–35, 39, 43–44, 46–47, 49, 51, 59, 61
lizards, 5–7, 9, 14, 15, 16, 17, 22–25, 27, 30, 35–36, 39, 46–48, 71, 81, 83, 86, 93–94
  anoles, 15, 27
  bearded dragons, 5–9, 27, 33, 35, 46–48, 60–61, 82, 97
  blue-tongued skinks, 46–48, 82
  chameleons, 22, 24, 27, 39, 71, 81, 85
  geckos, 17, 22–23, 24, 32, 46–48, 60–61, 71, 81–82, 83
  iguanas, 22, 30, 39, 46, 71, 85
  Komodo dragons, 22, 96
  monitor lizards, 15, 27, 46
  tegus, 27, 46
London Zoo, 27

Mesozoic era, 13
metabolic bone disease, 38, 39
MorphMarket, 56, 58

neutering, 39
new species, 15
New Zealand, 14
North American Reptile Breeders Conference & Trade Shows, 56, 67

omnivores, 23, 25, 35, 48

pens, 31, 49
permits, 11, 30, 70, 76–77
pet stores, 7, 55–56, 58, 60–61, 66, 85, 89
Practical Reptile Keeping, 66

releasing reptiles, 77, 79, 82, 84–86
ReptiFiles, 66–67
Reptile Awareness Day, 99
Reptile Networks, 66
Reptile Rescue Center, 86
Reptiles Magazine, 66
rescues, 7–8, 60, 82, 86, 87–88, 98

salmonella, 73
skin, 15, 17, 22, 24, 34–35, 38, 92
snakes, 5–7, 9, 14, 16–19, 20–21, 23, 25, 30, 32, 35–36, 41–46, 60–62, 66–67, 71, 74–77, 81, 86, 92, 94–96, 99
  anacondas, 19, 42, 74
  boas, 19, 41, 43, 45, 77, 81
  corn snakes, 41, 43–45, 60, 77, 86
  pythons, 15, 19, 20–21, 41–42, 44–45, 60, 74, 77, 82, 86–87
social media, 55, 63, 97–98, 99
Society for the Study of Amphibians and Reptiles, 64
solitary, 35
spaying, 39
substrate, 32–33, 39, 43, 47, 51, 59, 61

tails, 15, 20, 50
temperature, 5–6, 10, 11, 16, 24, 32–33, 37, 43–44, 47–49, 51, 56, 59, 61
Temple of Pythons, 20–21
thermometers, 8, 33, 56
tongues, 9, 17, 18, 23, 48
Torrini, Lori, 66–67
turtles and tortoises, 6, 9, 14–16, 24–27, 30–31, 35–36, 49, 50, 51–53, 60–61, 73, 81, 93–94, 96
  African spurred tortoises, 49
  box turtles, 49, 51, 53
  red-eared slider turtles, 27
  Russian tortoises, 49, 50, 51
  sea turtles, 15, 25–26, 53

veterinary care, 7, 30, 33, 35–39, 62, 64, 66, 76, 86, 88–89
vivariums, 7–9, 31–33, 35, 37, 39, 43–45, 47, 49, 51–53, 56, 59, 91

water, 7, 14, 18, 22, 24, 35–36, 43, 48, 50, 51–53
wild-caught reptiles, 11, 27, 69–71, 74, 79–82, 88, 97
wildlife trafficking, 74, 80–82, 97
World Wildlife Fund, 73

YouTube, 61, 67

ABOUT THE AUTHOR

Yvette LaPierre lives in North Dakota with her family and writes and edits books and articles for children and adults.